Amazing Dinosaurs Coloring Book
For Kids Age 4 to 8

This Book Belongs To :

Magical Colors

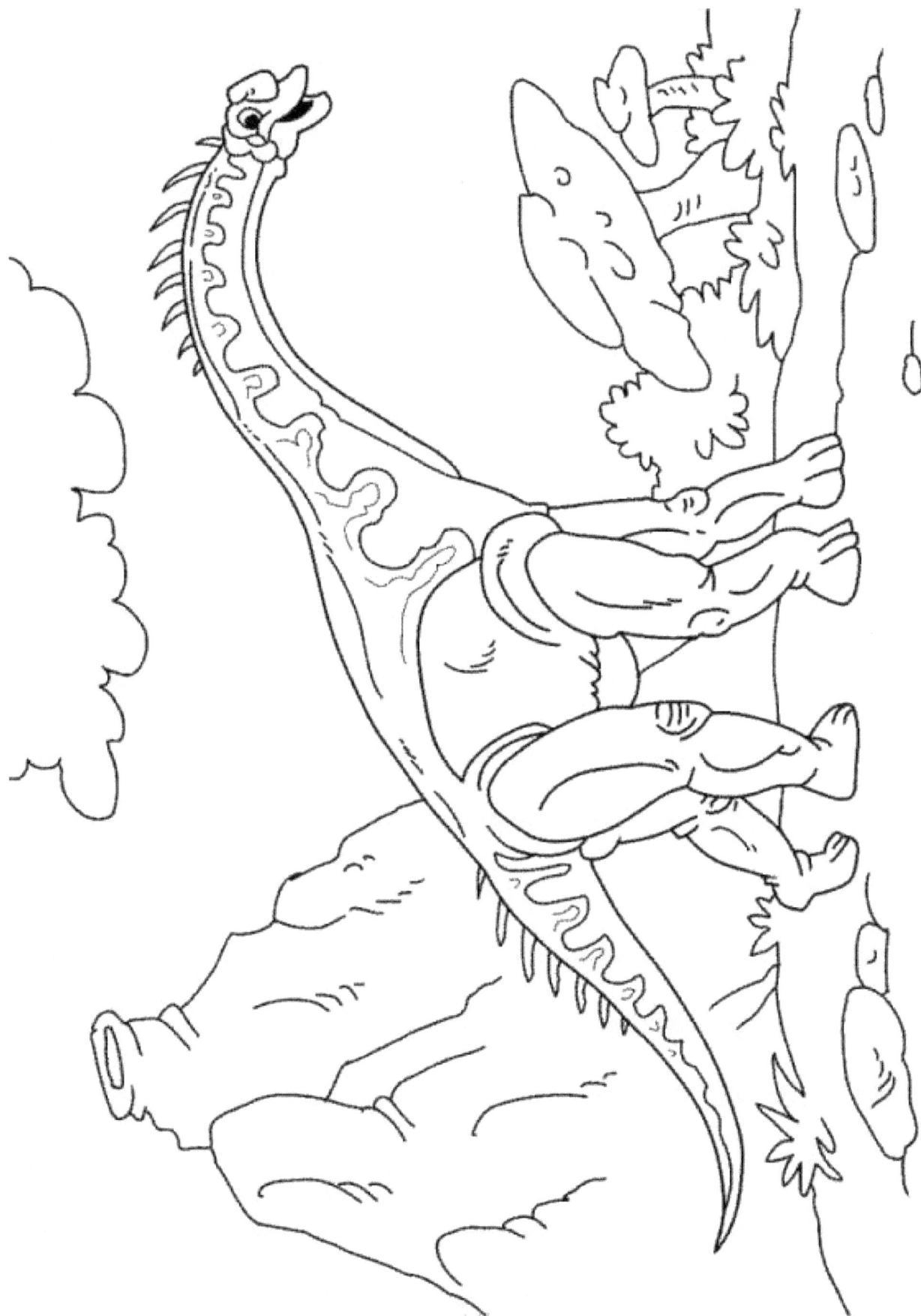

WE'RE HONORED

There's a lot of choices out there but you singled us out and that means a lot.

We just want to express how much we appreciate your purchase.

We love our customers dearly and your feedback is so helpful for us to hear.

Please let us know how you like our book at:

magicalcolors20@gmail.com

/magicalcolorsforkids

/magicalcolors20

A great Big Thank You!

CPSIA information can be obtained
at www.ICGtesting.com
Printed in the USA
BVHW050922271221
624880BV00016B/712

9 781716 271199